Recipe for Life

Recipe for Life

Soul-Stirring Stories from the Heart of Married Couples

Stanley and Omega Jones

XULON PRESS

Xulon Press
2301 Lucien Way #415
Maitland, FL 32751
407.339.4217
www.xulonpress.com

Unless otherwise indicated, Scripture quotations taken from the New
King James Version (NKJV). Copyright © 1982 by Thomas Nelson,
Inc. Used by permission. All rights reserved.

Printed in the United States of America.

ISBN-13: 978-1-6305-0639-1

This book is dedicated in memory of our parents Stanley Jones Sr., Mansoor and Ameenah Salahuddin

ACKNOWLEDGEMENTS

All honor and glory are due to our Lord and Savior Jesus Christ, who through the Word of God confirmed that it was time to write this book. We thank God for His provisions, direction, and the power and presence of the Holy Spirit who speaks life into visions.

We are so grateful to all who have played a part in this project, for your love, prayers, and spiritual guidance. To our contributors, Deacon William and Reverend Belynda Gentry, Anthony and Lisa Jones, Majid and Alesha Salahuddin, Corey and Shaunda Bellamy, Tyrone and Akilah Jefferson, this project would not be what God wanted it to be without your willingness and transparency. Thank you for sharing your stories. We love you all dearly.

Thank you to our former Pastor and First Lady, the late Rev. Dr. Weldon G. Thomas and Marilyn Thomas for your amazing counsel and for marrying us in 1997.

To one of our spiritual parents and former Pastor and First Lady, Reverend Dr. Wardell and Dr. Bester Bonner, we are so grateful for you and the love that you have shown us for over twenty years. Thank you for always being there for us.

Thank you to our Pastor John K. Jenkins, Sr., and First Lady Trina Jenkins for your biblical teachings and transparency, honesty, and for being godly examples for marriages. The teachings have inspired us, and we have applied the teachings to our lives and are now sharing those teachings with others through this book.

To our parents, Marian Jones and the late Stanley Jones Sr., Rasheeda Salahuddin and the late Mansoor and Ameenah Salahuddin—none of this would be possible without you. Thank you for all that you have provided and poured into us. The many sacrifices you made for us throughout our lives can never be repaid. Your love and teachings have not been in vain. You are the best parents that any child could have.

To our siblings, Shonte, Deanna, Amanda, Tasha, Sarah, Ashly, Michael, Tamar, Omar, Akbar, Bilal, Eli, Majid, Mansoor (deceased), Paulette, Yasmin, Shuron, Muriel and Farida, thank you for your encouragement, love, and support.

Finally, to our beautiful daughters and granddaughter, Ayesha, Jamilah, Asiah, Taelor, and Sydney. We are so proud of you. You have become beautiful women, and we are so honored to be your parents. Remember to always keep God first in all that you do. To our first granddaughter Sydney, GiGi and Bishop love you dearly; you are so bright, and we can't wait to see how God is going to use you. Continue to be a mighty prayer warrior. The best is yet to come!

Table of Contents

FOREWORD

Having known Stanley and Omega for more than twenty years, starting in their young adult years, I feel confident that I know them well enough to say that they are great assets to proclaiming the Good News—the message of the kingdom of Christ. It's a blessing to be counted among those who have provided spiritual guidance to them. They demonstrate that they are comfortable in their own skin, have genuine respect for each other's role in the family, and always encourage one another in validating and utilizing their unique spiritual gifts and career talents to God's glory and service to humankind.

As partners in the faith, they taught their children by word and deed the virtues of seeking God as the ultimate source in all life's relationships, whether at home, work, school, church, or play. Likewise, with family, extended family, and friends, they share with deep humility, their zeal that you can live in victory if you, *"Trust in the Lord with all your heart, And lean not on your own understanding; In all your ways acknowledge Him, And He shall direct your paths."* (Prov. 3:5-6). At the same time, they are dedicating their lives to the Lord's service at home and in the mission field. A unique quality they possess is their innate ability to express their voice as one voice, give a voice to the five contributing couples, and empower them to share their own marriage journey and how they applied the five core beliefs.

Just as Stanley and Omega, we would like you to be more comfortable, open, and compassionate in your marriage. Are you willing to tell the truth about who you are in Christ and your relationships? How can you find your own voice in this dialogue, thus giving one voice as a continuing conversation to this essential discussion?

Your thirst for answers will be satisfied as you journey through *Recipe for Life*, a compelling collection of stories and testimonies from married couples sharing their innermost thoughts and feelings about their marriage journey. In poignant language and collectively, yet in one voice, these couples, with supporting scriptures, create a climate of motivation that excites.

Their journey electrifies the reader as they show us how to prayerfully and meditatively stir in the five (5) "I" ingredients—iBelieve (Rom. 10:9); iSurrender (Rom. 12:1-2); iLove (John 3:16); iHope (Ps. 147:11); iTrust (Prov. 3:5-6). They echo that these ingredients are undisputable essentials to fulfilling the laws of God in a Christian marriage. They tastefully identify the ingredients and term them five (5) core beliefs that contribute to a fulfilled life in Jesus Christ and as life-giving words of God in the bond of marriage.

Allow your five senses of touch, taste, hear, see, and feel to savor their experiences. You will be able to interpret what is happening in your life and with others, and you can even commit or recommit to the "I" ingredients to make your marriage more fulfilling. The experience itself is a reward.

Hence, the dialogues collected in *Recipe for Life* reflect their insatiable yearning to share their journey with a wider audience by making a worthwhile contribution to the controversial conversations that are taking place in our society around the sacredness of marriage as ordained by God in His Word. The ideas that are promoted in *Recipe for Life* all lead the reader back to the need to think in the "I" way. It is personal, yet in marriage, it must be a partnership journey—both partners working together in seeking God in the richness and fullness of everything they face in the arena called life. They seek God's revelation through the Holy Spirit by praying, meditating, and studying the inerrant Word of God in their marriage for decision-making. You too can experience that blessed assurance the couples so vividly describe in *Recipe for Life*. It is in surrendering our total selves to God that we experience the depth and majesty of His power as we apply His teachings to our marriages and in all our relationships. May God bless you in this walk with Stanley and Omega. Enjoy the journey to wholeness in Christ!

Dr. Bester Joyce Davis Bonner

INTRODUCTION

October 25, 1997, is when it all began. Over the past twenty-two years, God has blessed us tremendously and placed so many people in our paths that have been a blessing to us and those we have been able to bless. In 2007, God spoke to Omega through a dream to start Through Faith Ministry. Although it took eleven years to officially launch the ministry, it did not stop us from spreading the gospel and impacting lives throughout the world. The goal of this ministry is to use tools and resources to spread the gospel of Jesus Christ, impacting lives for Christ, and to leave a legacy for our children's children, as stated in Proverbs 13:22, *"A good man leaves an inheritance to his children's children."* God is working through us and preparing us for this moment.

HIS STORY

Growing up in rural Buckingham County, Virginia, a two-parent household with six sisters and no brothers, how did I make it? It was not easy for my dad and I with all those women. Although Buckingham is a very small town, I am grateful to call it home and grateful I was obedient in leaving. Being in high school was one of the most memorable times for me. Sometimes I was the class clown, and other times, I felt like an outsider.

Looking back, I realize all the missed opportunities, the gifts and talents I did not use that God had given me. Graduating in 1987 and then joining the U.S. Marine Corps was another great highlight of my life. The Marine Corps afforded me the opportunity to travel the world and experience so many different cultures. Serving my country during the time of peace and war was very dear to my heart. **SEMPER FI!**

Watching my parents growing up, I knew marriage would be in my future. I wanted to have a family one day, but I knew I had to break some generational curses. I now understand how my parents' generation is completely different than mine, the way they were raised and the way their parents were raised. I wanted to be a good provider, be active in church, and openly express my love for my wife and family. Although I desired those things, life was not that easy. After joining the Marine

Corps and four years traveling the world, I lost connection with friends, family and really felt like an outsider. As I reflect on those years, I was depressed and did not know it. My life was not aligned with God. I wandered in the wilderness and did not know that I was lost.

I witnessed both of my grandparents being married for over fifty (50) years, and my parents were married for fifty-four (54) years. I was inspired and wanted to continue that legacy. Being alone was not an option for me; I wanted to spend the rest of my life with someone. In the mid-1990s, I reached a low point in my life with relationships and realized that in order for me to be all that I could be, I needed a wife to help me through this process. Thank God I found Omega; better yet, thank God that Omega found me.

My desire to have a wife lined up with Scripture. Proverbs 18:22 states, "*He who finds a wife finds a good thing, and obtains favor from the Lord.*" Genesis 2:18 states, "*The Lord God said, 'It is not good for the man to be alone. I will make a helper suitable for him.'*" I was destined to be married and stood on this word.

In 1995, I rededicated my life to the Lord, and God began to order and direct my steps. One year later, I met the love of my life, and my life has never been the same. Tramaine Hawkins song "Change" describes completely what happened to me, "A change, a change has come over me. He changed my life and now I'm free." (Hawkins, Tramaine. Changed. https://www.youtube.com/watch?v=7Kymk9f2TNQ. July 28, 2009)

HER STORY

Born to Paul Bolding and Doris Clomax, my story is so much different than Stanley's. I was born and raised in Washington, DC, and was number eleven of fourteen brothers and sisters. When I was born, there were four older sisters and six older brothers living at home. I often tell the story that my parents named me Omega because they thought I was going to be the last child, but there were three after me! So, there is no Alpha in the family, just an Omega. That story always makes people laugh!

My parents were both born and raised in Christian homes. I understand that when they met, my mother was a recent divorcee with two boys, who are my two older brothers, and she had converted to Islam. My father, who had one child out of wedlock, met my mother in Washington, DC, and he also converted to Islam. They became very active in the Nation of Islam, and my parents later changed their names to Mansoor and Ameenah Salahuddin. They were married for twenty-three years before my mother passed away in 1978.

I lost my mother at the age of eleven, and my life has never been the same. At the time of my mother's death, I was one of the oldest siblings living at home and took on the responsibilities of a mother to my three younger siblings. I experienced not having what other children or my friends had, as well as having to give up my teenage years for the sake of the family. Although times were very hard for my family, I graduated from my sixth-grade class with high honors.

Growing up in a very strict, disciplined, and religious home, I had never been on a date, nor had a boyfriend. My older brothers and sisters attended a Muslim school and traditionally graduated as early as sixteen years of age. Culturally, the girls in my family did not date. If you were interested in someone, the person of interest would talk with the parents, and the next thing you knew, they were married at a young age. I do not have memories of my mother having conversations with me about sex, contraception, drugs, alcohol, or dating, because I was so young when she passed away. Those topics were taboo. When I got a little older, we were told things like, "Keep your legs closed," or, "You are too young to date."

When I was young and I saw young ladies with babies in strollers, I used to say, "I would never get pregnant," or, "That will never happen to me." Until one day it did! I was sixteen, pregnant, and I thought my life was over. I had considered myself a good girl, who would go to college after high school and live the American dream. But, you see, I, like many of us, messed up at a young age. I did not treat sex as it should be, as sacred. A lot of relationships do not last because they start the wrong way, based on sex! I was young and naïve, not knowing that entering into sex before marriage sets in motion, problematic relationships.

Despite the odds of being a teenage mother, I continued to excel in high school and did not let having a child discourage me from doing my best and graduating on time with my peers. I was fortunate to participate in a cooperative education program which placed me in a federal government agency while earning high school credits. This part-time employment led to full-time federal government employment. Since I was unable to attend college, this was truly a blessing, that I was able to care for my daughter.

In spite of life circumstances and the difficult challenges of raising a child, I never gave up on striving to be successful, having a spirit of excellence, or providing for my family. I persevered through trials while maintaining my faith in God. I am thankful for a thirty-five-year public service career, an amazing family, four beautiful daughters, one grand-daughter, and a wonderful, loving, and supportive husband. I am a living testimony that being a teenage mother does not have to be the end of your life. I am reminded, "Don't give up on God because He won't give up on you."

Even during my wilderness experience, God still had His hands on my life. The Bible teaches in Psalm 34:18-19 that *"The Lord is near to those who have a broken heart, and saves such as have a contrite spirit. Many are the afflictions of the righteous, But the Lord delivers him out of them all."*

Before I met Stanley, I had been divorced for about three years. I was not saved when I was previously married. It was a marriage that was not God-ordained, and I experienced physical, mental, and emotional abuse. It was a really dark time in my life, I felt alone and was not able to share with my father, brothers, or sisters what was really going on in my marriage.

I had decided after the divorce that I was going to focus on myself and raising my two daughters. We moved in with one of my sisters, and I was able to save money to buy my first home.

The girls and I did not have a church home. We would periodi-cally visit Galilee Baptist Church in Suitland, MD, or Full Gospel AME Church in Temple Hills, MD, but I was not ready to commit to joining a church. I had so many things going on in my mind from my upbringing and Islamic principles that I learned growing up that were confusing to me. Even during that time in my life, I felt God's covering. When I visited churches, I always heard a word or a song that would inspire me or bring conviction. Little did I know, it was the Holy Spirit speaking directly to me. Now, I understand what the scripture says about God's Word does not return to Him void. (Is. 55:11).

I remember one night in my sister's basement, I was having a really tough time with trying to balance my life. I cried out to the Lord, and I asked Him to save me. I asked God to send me the mate that He would desire for me. I remember when I got up from praying, I felt a release. I surrendered my life and God save me.

It was only by the grace of God and a divinely-appointed time that the Lord blessed me with my God-fearing husband, Stanley. You see, like Stanley, I also lived in a period of depression during my life. I now realize that God had to take me through, and bring me out, to guide me through this life's journey.

OUR STORY

It was July 1996, at Prince George's Community College, Summer Session II, Speech 101 class, the true beginning. Little did we know what God had in store for us. We spent six weeks in Speech 101. One version of the story is that Omega was stalking Stanley, but if the truth be told, Stanley had his eyes on Omega. "She was so beautiful and sexy, and I remember exactly what she was wearing and how she wore her hair (A white dress, lime green accents, and lime green sandals—man I'm good)."

On the last day of class, I finally got up enough nerve to approach Omega. "I was nervous, but I knew this was my last chance to get her number, so I went for it." Omega was very receptive to my invitation for lunch, and our first date was at my company's annual cookout. After about a month of dating, I called Omega at work and told her that I loved her and that I was going to marry her.

Of course, I did the right thing and asked permission from Omega's parents for their blessings. Six months later, we were engaged, and on October 25, 1997, we became one. A country boy and a city girl connecting to form a perfect union in the sight of God.

Oh, and did I mention that Omega has a voice like an angel? She serenaded me at our wedding with her rendition of Whitney Houston's song, "I Believe in You and Me." It was so beautiful, a day we will always remember.

Although we formed a perfect union, we were a blended family. Omega had two daughters, Ayesha and Jamilah, and I had one daughter, Asiah. Blending families together was not an easy thing; it was a lot of work. The girls had experienced some form of trauma from our past relationships. One of the things we agreed to before we were married was that we not use the term "step-parents." This was an important piece in helping our families become one. We stressed to our children that it was not "them" or "my" mom or "my" dad—it was "us," "our" mom and "our" dad.

Setting these boundaries and expectations with the girls was critical for us to have a healthy family. We tried to model before them, with the help of God, the importance of having a personal relationship with Jesus Christ, serving in the community, treating others like you want to be treated, having integrity, having a good work ethic, praying for a God-sent husband, getting a college education, keeping up a home, and making home-cooked meals. With God's grace and mercy, none of the girls were teen mothers, and by May of 2021, all of the girls will have graduated from college with bachelor's and master's degrees. To God be the glory!

God continues to amaze us and open many doors for us, and in 2012, God called Stanley to finish his education in preparation for ministry. While Omega had always had a passion for education, she decided to take the journey with him. The journey was not easy as working adults raising a family, having three daughters in college, and caring for each other's needs as husband and wife. This sacrificial love between us was a commitment that we made to one another, and we are eternally grateful to God for seeing us through.

Omega was blessed to complete her Bachelor of Science degree in Biblical Studies with honors in December 2013. However, she wanted to continue to encourage Stanley in his education, so she decided to wait until he completed his degree in December 2014. Being able to walk together not only brought completion to what we started in 2012, but it further strengthened our marriage and serves as an example to other married couples. In 2015, God blessed us to walk together at the graduation ceremony for Lancaster Bible College. To God be the glory for all of the great things He has done and will continue to do is our testimony. We are standing on God's promises in Philippians 1:6, "*...being confident of this very thing, that he who has begun a good work in you will complete it until the day of Jesus Christ.*"

STORIES FROM OUR HEART

You may wonder, what stories or challenges could the Joneses share with us? Just like all of us, we have had good times, bad times, struggles, and heartaches. But we did not allow these times and struggles to define us or persuade us from the commitment we made to each other and to God. We vowed to love each other in sickness and health, for richer or poorer, until death do us part. We pray that our stories will encourage you along this journey.

Unchartered Waters

Just when you think you have figured out how to love and please each other in marriage, you find that there are highs and lows and different seasons you will encounter. We have been in seasons where we have grieved the loss of loved ones, experienced financial crises, and had challenging job situations, health crises, and family drama. I remember Pastor Jenkins saying in one of his sermons, "You have to experience a person in season and out of season before making the commitment to enter into a lifelong relationship." I believe we have confidence in each other in knowing that we will be there for one another through any situation, 'til death do us part.

There was a season in our marriage where we experienced unchartered waters. We had become too familiar with each other, and intimacy was not where it should have been. We took each other for granted and assumed that we were pleasing one another. We were involved in ministry, but not working on our first ministry, which after God is each other. Ministry and work for Stanley was his number one focus, trying to do and be everything for all people. Stanley was so consumed with success that he did not realize how he was impacting me and the family. His priorities were not in order. He leaned on his own understanding instead of leaning on the Lord. Although he was a great provider, he was missing the mark. Because he was not in tune to the Holy Spirit, he could not see how I was hurting inside.

This season of our life was challenging, I did not have anyone to talk to about how I was feeling. Each time we tried to talk about these unchartered waters and our level of intimacy, the conversations never went anywhere. We were in our flesh. One day while I was driving to work, I was introduced to the Family Life radio station, FM 105.1. This is an amazing Christian radio station. I would listen to couples speak about their challenges and how they overcame, and God spoke to me about surrendering my will completely to Him and placing my marriage in His hands. I began to read and study the Word and was reminded that Stanley is God's son and I am His daughter. I was convicted by the scripture Matthew 6:33, *"But seek first his kingdom and his righteousness, and all these things will be given to you as well."*

We needed to trust God to direct our paths and show us the next steps to take in moving our marriage forward. Prior to joining First Baptist Church of Glenarden (FBCG), we started attending the FBCG Couples Fellowships.Under the leadership of Reverends Skip and Beverly Little, we were reminded that a threefold cord is not quickly broken, as stated in Ecclesiastics 4:12. We needed each other, but more importantly, we needed God to be at the center of our marriage. We recommitted ourselves to each other and after joining FBCG, vowed to put God first, our marriage second, family, ministry and then work. One of the most important decisions we made was to not put ministry before our marriage. We agreed to participate in one ministry at a time so that we would not get distracted by serving and forget about what's most important, our first ministry, home. This has been big for our marriage. You can't be all that God has called you to be if you forget about your first ministry. How do you give more to others and neglect your first ministry, your spouse and family? Being intentional and deliberate helped us calm the unchartered waters with God being the Captain of the ship.

Family Tests

One of the biggest tests early on in our marriage was dealing with baby mommy drama. "For all the brothers out there, and know what I am talking about, say 'AMEN.'" For almost thirteen years, it was a constant battle. One thing we have done is take great care of our children. However, having to fight in the courtroom on numerous occasions for my rights was draining on us and the family. We felt like at every turn, the enemy was trying to do everything to hurt us and our family. In 2000, we sold our townhome in Landover Hills, MD, and were waiting for our home to be built in Upper Marlboro, MD. Although I was paying my child support and arrears, they were not satisfied. They obtained an outside agency to come after the arrears of $12,000 to stop us from moving into our new home. This was devastating to us. We did not know how we could come up with $12,000 in a way that would not impact our ability to close on the home. Mad and pissed off, we were worried that we would be homeless. Fortunately, two days before the money was due, I was able to get a loan from the company I worked for to pay the arrears.

We were tested on many fronts during this time; it strained us emotionally. This roller coaster ride was long and frustrating. Although there was a court order in place, there were numerous violations of the court order. We remember one Thanksgiving we arrived to pick up our daughter and the house was dark. They had left and gone out of town with no regard for the court order. This moment was so painful; when we look back, we are so grateful to God that He sustained us through this and so many other times. When our daughter turned eighteen, it was a relief for us and the family. She was able to make her own decisions—what a glorious day! We did not lean on God fully, but can look back and see how the hand of God was upon us. Even when it looked hopeless, we did not lose hope.

Another family crisis that tested our faith was when our youngest daughter was born two months premature. As we mentioned, when we met, we were a blended family. A year after we were married, we thought we would try to have a son. Yes, Stanley was surrounded by girls, and I was hoping to give him a son. When I found out I was pregnant, we were both ecstatic. The girls were happy because this would really bind our family together. Everything was going well in the pregnancy. It was in the summer of 1999, and we were spearheading a Crab Feast at our former church. Well, I absolutely love crabs, and I, of course, indulged. The day following the event, I notice that our daughter was not kicking as much, and I was worried, but did not tell Stanley. I monitored the activity overnight. The next day was Monday, and I was at work and our daughters movement was still abnormal, so I called Stanley at work and told him. He said not to worry and to call the doctor. The doctor's advice was to drink something cold and sugary and see if the movement picked up. Our daughter was still not moving as much, so the doctor told me to come in. Upon my arrival, I was immediately given a sonogram, where I could see that our daughter was visibly sluggish. Stanley and I prayed, and we did worry. I was checked in, and the monitoring continued. The doctors were running tests, and by Wednesday of that week, they were scheduling me for an emergency caesarean. Our daughter was originally due in November; however, our daughter was born two months early. We went through several iterations of names, and we ended up naming her Taelor Noel Jones.

Taelor had to stay in the Neonatal Intensive Care Unit at the Washington Hospital Center for thirty days. We had no other option but to trust, surrender, believe, hope, love, and pray during this season. For thirty days, we traveled back and forth to the hospital center to take breast milk and feed Taelor. We would visit her at the hospital with the girls after church on Sundays and talk to her as the nurses instructed us to do. After thirty days in the hospital and after running many tests, the doctors informed me that Taelor's health was impacted by something called Listeria.

The bacteria came from whatever I had eaten the weekend before. Although, I was not sick, it made Taelor sick while she was in my womb. The emergency caesarean was to save her life so that they could treat her out of the womb. I am getting emotional recounting this crisis, but I am reminded of Jeremiah 29:11, *"For I know the plans I have for you,' declares the Lord, 'plans to prosper you and not to harm you, plans to give you hope and a future.'"* Stanley and I believe that God took us through that season in our marriage to strengthen us and to be an encouragement to other couples that God is with us and that He will never leave us nor forsake us.

Financial Tests

What marriage has not experienced some type of financial test? Well, we were not taught the true value of money and how to use money to your advantage. Not having those basic foundational principles negatively impacted our marriage in the early years. As mentioned, Omega is from a family of fourteen, and Stanley's is from a family of six. Of course, Omega's father worked hard all of his life, sometimes holding two jobs to care for his family, and Stanley's dad was the primary income earner. Neither of us were born into wealth, and we saw firsthand how our parents had to struggle. As the head of the household, I did not truly understand the importance of saving and, more importantly, having a budget. So, instead of me taking an active role in the process, I spent and left the hard work for Omega to work it out.

In 2004, life caught up with me, with us. After changing jobs three times in a span of five years, there was no money saved, but debt increased. Working in the private sector has its pluses and minuses; stability was not one of the pluses. One saving grace was that Omega worked for the federal government and we could count on her income. We were actively involved in our church, but not consistent tithers, and looking back at this time, we consumed a lot.

The early part of 2004, we were having a very hard time paying our mortgage and other obligations. After three months of missing our mortgage payments, we opened an envelope from our mortgage company to find a notice to foreclose on our home. This was one of the scariest times in our marriage.

We did not have any other couples to talk this through with. We thank God that we did not blame each other. Our trust in God was tested. All the things that could happen were on our mind—losing our home, being homeless, the embarrassment, shame, it was a heavy load to bare. The financial strain on our marriage was real and hard.

We finally came to our senses and realized that God would not put more on us than we could bear. We believed that God did not want us to be homeless and that He did not bring us this far to leave us. We sought the Lord and asked God for His deliverance, and He did just that. Family and friends came through for us.

This experience opened our eyes to how delicate life is if you are not financially prepared. Although we started our marriage with one bank account, that was not enough. We did not put in place sound financial practices; we spent and spent and spent.

Finally, Stanley started to be actively engaged in our finances. He developed a budget to track our income and expenses and how the money was being spent. We sit down now and go over the budget every two weeks to ensure we stay on track. This has helped our marriage tremendously, making financial decisions together and not in isolation.

Along our journey, Satan was still busy. In 2012, Satan tried again to attack us through our finances. Stanley transitioned from the private sector to the federal government. He went from being an executive (six-figure salary) to a GS-12, Step 1. From the office to the cubicle is what he always says. Before he accepted the job, Omega and Stanley's dad reminded him that everything was going to be okay, and to accept the job.

This was challenging, to say the least, but we never wavered in our faith that God was able, if we continued to believe, surrender our will, love each other, keep hope in Christ, and trust that God would provide.

Although we kept the faith, we wondered how long it would be before God would answer our prayers, how long would we be able to sustain this large pay cut. We did not stop praying; we continued to give what we were able to give, and because of our unwavering faith, God showed up in a supernatural way. In just eight (8) months, God elevated Stanley from a GS-12 to a GS-14. From the cubicle to the office, look at God.

God did not stop there. Two years later, God elevated him to director. When we got out of the way and fully surrendered everything to God as it says in Romans 12:1-2 and we put our full trust in God (Prov. 3:5-6), then God began to move on our behalf.

We could have taken matters into our own hands, but the results would have been different. The lessons we learned early on in marriage prepared us for times like this and others. It is when your faith is tested and your back is up against the wall that the true you is on display. Can God trust you to withstand the test? Or will you run in defeat?

These events and others over the past twenty-two years has shaped us, and we are making progress to meet our financial goal of being debt free. We are grateful to the teachings of our Pastor, John K. Jenkins Sr. and FBCG on financial management, tithing and that God does not want us to be borrower to the lender (Prov. 22:7, "*The rich rules over the poor, and the borrower is servant to the lender*"). God wants us to live a victorious life, free from the financial burdens that weigh us down or distract us from our destiny.

THROUGH FAITH

We have learned so much along this journey. Our marriage has grown by being intentional and deliberate about our relationship. Investing in your marriage is a must. In 2017, we wanted to move our marriage to another level, so we enrolled in the Couples in Discipleship program at FBCG. This program was amazing. Not only were we able to connect with other couples, but we were drawn closer to each other. The course study was from the book *Sacred Marriage* by Gary Thomas. We applied what we learned regarding the importance of invoking God's sacred presence, knowing God's sacred mission, serving one another, falling forward in marriage, and dealing with sacred struggles. At the end of the session, a sacred ceremony was held, and the husbands washed their wives' feet. This ceremony sealed and modeled how Jesus served His disciples in John 13:14-15: *"Now that I, your LORD and Teacher, have washed your feet, you also should wash one another's feet. I have set you an example that you should do as I have done for you."* Life-changing.

As we said earlier, being intentional about participating in ministry was a decision we made when we joined FBCG, remembering that our first ministry was home. Our desire was that God would bless us to work and serve in ministry together. In 2014, God blessed us and honored our wishes. We serve in the International Missions Ministry together, and in 2017, God blessed us to serve as the new Director and Assistant Director of the ministry under the leadership of one of our spiritual parents, Reverend Belynda Gentry. It has been a blessing to work in ministry together, serving and impacting others. As we mentor other couples, we often share with them about how God is magnified as we serve in ministry together. God has blessed us to serve those in need both nationally and internationally in Peru. When we serve together, our lives are changed, and our marriage is strengthened by those who we encounter.

We believe that the greatest benefit for our marriage is to become better servants to each other. If we both pour our time and abilities into serving one another and continually investing in each other, the passion for each other grows. It means we are sharing our lives with each other, which brings us closer.

A husband and wife can consciously invite the presence of God into their marriage by being in a posture of prayer and being ready to serve each other. If we are in a posture of prayer, then we are always invoking the presence of God, and our hearts are open to hear from God through the Holy Spirit. When we are serving each other, it's serving God. We can't be all that our spouse desires for one day; it requires us to daily pursue each other, ensuring that we meet each other's needs. Marriage takes work and effort; it's not like our jobs that we leave every day and put on hold, marriage is 365.

When we consider making one of our favorite desserts, Omega's famous bean pies, in order for the pie to come together, you must have all of the ingredients—the navy beans, eggs, brown sugar, white sugar, cinnamon, pie crust, carnation milk, etc. When you strain the beans and mix all of the ingredients together and then bake the pie at 350 degrees, the pie comes out perfect every time. It will have you licking your fingers for more. Just like baking the bean pie and having all of the correct ingredients, the pillars of our ministry are focused on five (5) core beliefs, which we call the "Recipe for Life"—iBelieve, iSurrender, iLove, iHope, and iTrust. We believe that these key core beliefs or ingredients are the cornerstone for a fulfilled life in Christ Jesus. God wants marriages to be all that He has called them to be by believing, surrendering, loving, hoping, and trusting. God wants us to love each other unconditionally, as He has loved us. Daily, we draw on these ingredients for a purposeful life and marriage.

It is our hope that as you continue to read these soul-stirring stories from some amazing couples, you will be blessed, encouraged, and inspired to never give up on yourself or your marriage. *"Therefore, what God had joined together, let no man separate"* (Mark 10:9).

iBELIEVE

*"That if you confess with your mouth the Lord Jesus and believe
in your heart that God has raised Him from the dead,
you will be saved." (Romans 10:9 NKJV)*

Contributions by: Deacon William and Reverend Belynda Gentry

ABOUT US . . .

Before we get into the chapter ***iBELIEVE***, we want to tell you a little about us. We are William Jr. and Belynda Gentry. When we met, we were both divorcees with young children. Back then, the church didn't give us counseling or instructions on how to navigate blending the two families, etc. After a short time of "dating" (we didn't know any better), we married in June 1985. I wish I could tell you that it has been perfect since we said, "I do," but that would be far from the truth. The truth is that it was the beginning of seven very difficult years of blending two totally opposite families together. It was hard! In fact, it started on the day we came home from our honeymoon. Yes, you heard it right, the day we came home from our honeymoon. That day, we had one of the biggest fights ever! It was a communication issue—something, we believe, would have been addressed in counseling had we received some before we married. But, by God's grace, new mercies every morning, and constant prayer, we navigated through those tough first seven years. We are grateful that God is *still* keeping us, *still* teaching us, and *still* using us to help others who are where we have been and where we are.

Our blended family

William (Dad) brought Willie into the blend. Willie went from being an "only" child (as far as he knew) to being a "middle" child of three—from having all of the attention to having to share the attention, from having his own room to having to share it with an older brother, from very little structure and discipline to major structure and discipline. Blending was the hardest for Willie of all the children. It was very taxing on the entire family.

Belynda (Mom) brought Damian and De'Neen into the blend. Damian was excited about having a brother and someone to share the chores with. De'Neen wasn't liking having to share her mom with this man. Through much prayer and God's grace, we don't know when it happened, but we fully blended. We blended where it was from the heart, "This is my dad, my brother, my sister, my mom, our children." No "*step,*" just one totally blended family.

One last thing about our blend, remember I said that Willie thought he was an only child. He wasn't. He had an older blood sister that he didn't know about. After several years of marriage, Joyce, William's older daughter, reached out to us and connected to our family. This connection brought a daughter and a granddaughter into our lives. So, we started blending them into the family. Over time, with lots of love and patience, God gave us a seamless blended family for the ones who actually lived in the same house. There is still some disconnect with Joyce and the other kids.

We both are in full-time ministry and employed by the church. We hold key leadership positions; I (William) am employed as the CFO and serve in leadership as a deacon. Belynda is an associate pastor and the head of the missions department. That makes us "public figures" in the church. As such, it is very hard, if not impossible, to find people you can really talk to or be transparent with. So many people think we are, as they say, *"the cutest little couple"* or *"the perfect couple."* Perfect, we are far from that! People are drawn to us for advice and parental care. The funny thing for me (Belynda) is that even while I am hurting or we are going through something, the Lord gives me the ability to put "self" aside and call upon His wisdom and strength to be what He needs me to be for the hurting people that He sends to us. *iBELIEVE* these to be divine appointments. I find that they always strengthen me to go on and to know that in God's time, He will work things out for our good. To be honest, though, the wait sometimes is so hard!

Through these divine appointments, God has extended our family. Belynda's light has drawn nearly forty women under her wing—serving as their mentor or spiritual mother. Together, we mentor nearly thirty couples. Belynda always say that God has a sense of humor because we are going through our own ups and downs, but He keeps sending people our way and telling us, "Help them." So, that's what we do through the strength we get from Christ.

We have a para-church non-profit ministry that we founded in 2000. The ministry, *"Go Ye..." Ministries Worldwide, Inc.* ministers to both temporal and spiritual needs of God's people around the world and includes ministry to married couples.

iBELIEVE

Believing in God is the foundation of the Christian life and of a great Christ-centered marriage—a marriage that will stand the test of time. Simply put, both the husband and wife must believe in Jesus Christ—first as their personal Savior and then as their Lord. As the scripture says, *"that if you confess with your mouth the Lord Jesus and believe in your heart that God has raised Him from the dead, you will be saved."* (Romans 10:9) Without Jesus, marriage can never be all God intended; without Jesus, you can never experience true joy and contentment; without Jesus, your marriage can't represent what it is designed to declare to those around you who are void of a relationship with God through Jesus. Believing in Jesus embodies the Godhead—God the Father—God the Son—God the Holy Spirit.

Not only that, but when we believe in Jesus—when that belief is the foundation of who we are and all that we are—the fabric of our marriage will be governed by the Word of God. In other words, God is consulted and allowed to direct every decision, order every step, and control everything—word and deed is not for our glory but for His glory. He is in CONTROL 24/7, 365 days of every year!

iBELIEVE when our marriage is rooted and grounded in Christ:

- *We can get through anything in the strength of Christ.*
  The Bible says it this way, *"I can do all things through*

Christ Who strengthens me." (Philippians 4:13) Yes, we can wait on the Lord to cause change to occur. I know you are saying that it seems like you have been waiting for a long time. Don't quit on God; don't take matters into your own hands but draw on Christ's strength. Take your eyes off whatever it is that needs changing

> *You are stronger than you think when you operate in Christ's strength, not your own*

and focus on Jesus! Pray without ceasing for the will of God to be done. Guess what? Sometimes, God will show you, you—the area you have the power to change but haven't because you are waiting on Him to change what you are praying about. Don't be stubborn—no butts about it—believe that God can, and God will in His divine time get you through whatever you are going through.

Remember when we told you about our first seven years being extremely challenging? The blending of our family was creating tension like you would not believe. The kids begin to act out of character, blaming each other for everything that went wrong; they each wanted to leave and go live with their other parent, and the list goes on. That wasn't the only drama in our lives. Because we really didn't know each other, there were so many irritations for me (Belynda). A lot of it was from my upbringing and how I was trained to be very neat, clean, and orderly—also, learning very young to do everything from cleaning to cooking. William, on the other hand, had a stay-at-home mother who did so much for him, so he didn't do what I considered just basic house-keeping and common-sense chores. OMG, talk about creating blended stress; we had it, and it was continuous. It was only through the super-natural strength of Christ that we got through all of the differences that we brought into the marriage.

Don't misread what I just said. By no means are we *through*. In fact, as of this writing, we are in a winter season, and I am praying—hoping—that spring arrives soon! I can say that all of the tests and the trials, God used to draw us closer to Himself. He used them to strengthen us through Christ. *iBELIEVE* that God was growing us through our struggles; *iBELIEVE* that God used each test, trial, and struggle to increase our trust in Him and our dependency on Him; *iBELIEVE* God used everything we went through to manifest Christ's life in us; *iBELIEVE* God used those seasons in our lives to purify our hearts. Nobody wants to suffer. And, if the truth be told, everybody would opt out of suffering if they could. But suffering is a part of the transformation process of becoming who God sees us to be while *we are becoming* who He knows us to be. *iBELIEVE* suffering solid-ified our convictions and our resolve that divorce is not an option.

iBELIEVE when our marriage is rooted and grounded in Christ:

- *We can mirror Christ's love.* Read Ephesians 5:22-33. Our marriage should mirror the love that Christ has for the church—that sacrificial love—that love that keeps giving even when the other person may be selfish and only gives to get. Christ's love is so amazing—so unhindered by what people do or say. His love is so cap-tivating and so enveloping. There are so many people that have never seen the love of Christ in action. But God has given us the opportunity to show off that love—to show off Christ's character through our marriages. That is so amazing and such an honor. Jesus is our example. Like Paul, let's imitate Christ. When we do—when we mirror Christ's love, it's like a magnet—it has the ability to draw other couples to Him. It has the ability to pull couples up out of despair. Christ's love has the ability to stop couples from walking away and go to clinging and making a renewed commitment to honor their vows to one another and to God. We are

> *Jesus is our example! No need to look anywhere else – just imitate Him.*

not trying to paint a picture that this has been an easy walk. No, to the contrary, but it has been and is a growing faith walk.

iBELIEVE when our marriage is rooted and grounded in Christ:

- *We can be wise in every area of our life. iBELIEVE* that wisdom and understanding go hand in hand.

In the book of Proverbs, we are instructed to seek wisdom, given the benefits of wisdom, and told to get wisdom. The Bible says, *"Wisdom is the principle thing: Therefore, get wisdom. And in all your getting, get understanding."* (Proverbs 4:7) That sounds great, but where do we get the wisdom we need? Again, we turn to the Word of God to enlighten us on how to get wisdom. We get wisdom from God! *"If any of you lacks wisdom, let him ask of God, who gives to all liberally and without reproach, and it will be given to him*" (James 1:5). If you keep reading, God lets us know that we've got to ask in faith and without doubting. You can't believe and doubt at the same time. When you doubt, you are saying to God, *I don't really believe You can give me the wisdom I need to make wise decisions.* Another way of putting what doubt does is when you know you hear what God said but you say, *No way, God, it won't happen or she won't or he won't.* But if *iBELIEVE* 100 percent in the sovereignty of God, it never has to make sense and it can sound impossible, but if God is Who He says He is (He is), then we trust Him to do the seemingly impossible for us.

> *iBELIEVE 100 percent*
> *in the sovereignty of God*

We absolutely anticipate a miracle in every situation that He allows in our lives. *iBELIEVE* that He is up to something good out of everything we go through! Understand though that God's timing is not the same as ours. We can't rush Him to do it according to our concept of limits on time. Wait on Him and be of good courage; He will strengthen your heart. I don't know where this saying comes from, but you have heard it, *He may not come when you want Him, but He is right on time.* It's true! God is never late, even when we think He is.

Be wise in your finances, in how you treat each other, in how you communicate, and in how you love. Don't take anything for granted. Don't assume you know what each other wants or likes. Ask the right questions—ask until you get the right answers. Understand that everybody changes—change is constant. You may not be able to love your spouse the same way you did in the early years and get the same results, but use wisdom. And, fellas, dwell with her in understanding as she changes.

Closing thoughts around the *iBELIEVE* foundational scripture—the Word of God is the basis for our being. We *"confess with our mouth the Lord Jesus."* Without this confession, we are empty and void of true life. By making this confession, we receive abundant life as we begin our walk with the Lord Jesus Christ. But the salvation confession is only the beginning. It is confession that comes from the heart—the very core of our being—believing the saving work of Christ on the cross and His resurrection from the dead. It is what's in our heart that determines who we are. From the time we make this confession, we are changed from a sinner on our way to eternal damnation to a saint on our way to eternal peace. It is *through* Christ and *in* Christ that *iBELIEVE* you can have the main ingredient for the recipe for life.

We leave you with a list of *iBELIEVE* ingredients that, when applied, will help your marriage.

- *iBELIEVE* in God
- *iBELIEVE* in His Word
- *iBELIEVE* in our vows to God and each other
- *iBELIEVE* confession and repentance is ongoing until Jesus comes or we die
- *iBELIEVE* in imitating Christ
- *iBELIEVE* in God's timing
- *iBELIEVE* in God's transformational process being lifelong
- *iBELIEVE* it is all for God's glory

iSURRENDER

"I beseech you therefore, brethren, by the mercies of God, that you present your bodies a living sacrifice, holy, acceptable to God, which is your reasonable service. And do not be conformed to this world, but be transformed by the renewing of your mind, that you may prove what is that good and acceptable and perfect will of God."
(Romans 12:1-2 NKJV)

Contributions by: Tyrone and Akilah Jefferson

We met in 1995, the summer before we began our college years together. We were married following graduation and have built our lives together over the last two decades. We have two teenage children, and together we are a family of believers trying to do the Will of God for our lives.

Have you ever tried a new recipe and it didn't turn out quite the way you planned? Well, we have. We enjoy cooking together, and from time to time when following a recipe, we've decided not to add a specific item or maybe to add a little of this other thing we've come to trust or just maybe the kitchen tools we had weren't sufficient to get the job done. But, nonetheless, our kitchen has seen a cake or two that did not rise and a few way-too-spicy pasta dishes. When this happens to you, have you gone back and evaluated what went wrong? For us, we come back to the same conclusion each time. We inserted ourselves. We didn't follow the plan, didn't trust the process. We didn't surrender.

Merriam-Webster's online dictionary (2019) defines the word surrender as both a noun and a verb. As a noun, surrender is defined as "the action of yielding one's position, status, or the possession of something into the power of another." Surrendering is the voluntary cancellation of one's legal or rightful claim to control some item, action, or individual. As a verb, surrender means "to give up completely or agree to forgo especially in favor of another, to give oneself over to something (such as an influence), or to give oneself up into the power of another especially as a prisoner." (1. Merriam-Webster Online, s.v. "surrender," accessed on September 1, 2019, https://www.merriam-webster.com/dictionary/surrender)

Surrendering is an important part of the lives of believers. The Word of God is clear as it outlines that we are called to surrender many things to God, including (but not limited to) surrendering our lives (Rom. 12:1; Mark 8:35), surrendering our bodies (Rom. 6:13), surrendering our plans and goals (Prov. 3:5-7), surrendering our hearts (Job 11:13), and surrendering ourselves (Luke 9:23). Within this context, the act of surrendering is not simply accepting commands without protest. Instead, surrendering is when you accept being relieved of the burdens associated with direction-setting within your life. The act of letting go of the responsibility for setting the directions of our lives is a critical part of the process of sanctification that God takes each of us through. By first letting go of our desires and seeking only those things that God wants for us, we come into alignment with His will for our lives and His ultimate plan for our destiny. Unfortunately, most do not learn the value of surrender as quickly as we should, nor do we learn this lesson all at once. Within our own marriage, there have been many teachable instances where we, at the time, had not surrendered some area of our lives to God's will. Here, we will share our personal journeys of how God called each of us to surrender to His will for our lives.

Tyrone

I gave my life to Christ as a young adult. And while I firmly believed in the death, burial, and resurrection of Jesus Christ, I really didn't know how I should be living as a Christian. If you were to evaluate my life by the standard of the world, I was a "good" person. I was married and faithful to my wife. I was present and active in the lives of my children. I had a good job and oversaw the care, management, and protection of my household. I was doing pretty good, again, based on the world's standards. However, as a Christian, I am not supposed to live by the world's standards but by God's standard. If you were to evaluate my life according to the standard of God's Word, I came up very short in many key areas. But I didn't know that then. Not only did I not know where I was deficient, but I didn't even know that I was deficient to begin with. This is a dangerous condition to live in but, unfortunately, not an uncommon one. Some people live out their lives in this pattern of obliviousness, never understanding or questioning whether they are living their lives as God instructs His children through His Word. It is strange to say, but the best thing that could have happened to our family did on the day that God allowed everything to come crashing down, laying all of my deficiencies out in front of me to see.

Early in our marriage, we were a single-income family. I worked full-time while my wife stayed home caring for our children. We recognized this would place some limitations on our home and our shared earning potential, but at that time, we placed greater value on the benefits of having our children in our home (and not in daycare) over that of added income. And, as you might imagine, things were kind of "tight" financially, but I believed that we were alright and "making ends meet." Things were not alright. I am able to admit this now, but I was not a very good steward of my family's finances at that time. It was under my watch and approval, within this environment of an already reduced/restricted income, I "greenlighted" buying a house that we could not afford, buying a brand-new second car we really didn't need, relying (very) heavily on credit, and purchasing non-essential items and services before all monthly bills had been paid, all while taking no time to plan financially for our futures. Closer examination would show that we were in a situation where we had too much money going out and not nearly enough money coming in. Truth be told, with little to no savings, our financial situation was exceedingly tenuous. One or two major, unplanned expenses could have been disastrous, possibly leading to our family losing our home.

One Monday in the summer of 2006, a series of unplanned expenses would arrive at our doorstep. I remember the day very clearly. I had just pulled up in front of our house, home from a long day of work. I shut the car off, got out, and checked the mail. I was home alone, which was kind of unusual. Since I had some free time to myself, I got back in the car thinking that I might make a run to the store to grab some supplies I needed for work around the house. However, something (very likely the Holy Spirit) led me to look through the mail that I had received. There was some junk mail, a couple of magazines, some advertisements, and several plain-looking envelopes from companies with which we had open credit accounts. I started with the envelope from my primary credit card holder. It was an overdue notice, informing me that a penalty had been added to my account and that our monthly payment was due now. I was shocked and angry at the same time. I thought we kept up with our bills. Imagine my emotions as I opened the next three envelopes, seeing a series of overdue payment notices, requests for immediate payment, and threats of reporting my delinquencies to the credit bureaus. I was still shocked and angry, but now, I was also scared.

Though we did not keep a budget for our household expenses at that time, I knew that it was very likely that we could not afford to pay all of our regular bills as well as the accumulated penalty balances we had just received. This would, in all likelihood, mean that we would be defaulting on all of these accounts. As I sat there in the front seat of my car, a lot of thoughts passed through my mind. None of them were pleasant. I thought about having to sell off our things to pay bills. I thought about our utilities being cut off. I thought about having to potentially walk away from our home. I thought about what other people would think about me, that I was a failure or incompetent. Another recurring thought that I had that I finally verbalized was actually a question. It was short and straightforward: "God, how could You let this happen?" And in the very next moment, as though He was seated in the car right next to me, God replied, saying, "I did not do this. You did." And in the next few moments that followed His words, I saw images of every decision point (spiritual, financial, relational, or otherwise) in my past where I didn't seek God and how I had consistently put Him second, last, or nowhere in every part of my life.

To say that I was dumbfounded is a supreme understatement. It is still amazing to me when I think about it. God had just spoken to me and showed me how I had arrived at this point in my life. Reflecting on the situations and decisions that God showed me, I recognize now that my problems all stemmed from the fact that I had not surrendered myself to God. I was not living my life yielding to God's will, nor did I know or follow God's rules for living. Although I was saved and attended Sunday service regularly, I didn't study the Bible. I didn't serve in ministry. I didn't evangelize. I didn't fellowship with other Christians. I didn't tithe. I couldn't tell you the last time I had had communion. I was a Christian in name only, serving as lord and master over my life, living by my own whims, answerable and accountable to no one. In short, I hadn't surrendered any portion of my life to God. And the message I gleaned from God's vision was clear—the fact that I had lived a life where my desires were prioritized and not surrendered and submitted to the will of God had put my family in danger.

Sitting there in stunned silence by what God had shown me, I slowly accepted the truth, and I was embarrassed by my situation. Without any doubt, I was the author of my pain. And under the weight of this realization, I was intensely saddened and remorseful. After staring off into the distance for what felt like hours, a new question entered my mind. Although I did not have any "depth" of knowledge about God or the things of God, I did know (from a few sermons that I had heard) that God had a penchant for repairing the irreparable; He is a waymaker. Knowing His reputation and knowing that He was listening, I spoke aloud, "God, can You please fix this?" That time, God didn't reply verbally. Instead, an image came into my mind. I remembered seeing an advertisement for Bible study in the announcements before church the previous week. It was on Tuesday night at 7:00 pm. Without saying so, God was telling me He could fix this but I would need to trust Him and voluntarily surrender to His shepherding and guidance.

> *"The Lord is my shepherd; I shall not want."*
> *Psalm 23:1*

This scripture means that God is my leader and my provider. As my leader, I do what God instructs me to do. And as my provider, I have what He wants me to have. Here, confronted with this image of Bible study, God wanted to see if I would submit to His leadership, surrendering my desires and deferring to His plan. Convicted by what I had seen, I said aloud, "Yes, God." And the next day, following the direction given to me by God, my family and I went to Bible study.

In the years since this day, things have gotten much better for our family. Our outlook, both spiritually and financially, has drastically improved. As a family, we still attend church regularly, and we all serve in multiple ministries. However, now my wife and I both study the Bible and have personal devotionals. We have both attended personal and couple-focused discipleship training. We evangelize and fellowship with other Christians. We tithe faithfully and attend communion monthly. Also, we attend couples fellowship teachings and events to continually grow and develop our relationship. While it has taken time, God has been faithful. By His blessing, we've closed all of our credit accounts and have had the funds to eliminate nearly all of our outstanding credit card debt. And though we're still primarily a single-income family, God has blessed us to see many increases and meet all of our family's necessities and even some of our desires. And although things are not perfect, God gets all the glory from everything in my life (no matter how big or small). Since being convicted by God, I've worked diligently to trust in Him with all my heart, leaning not to my own understanding, acknowledging Him in all things, allowing Him to direct my path.

The lesson here is a simple one. In this life, we are granted the liberty to choose for ourselves. We are free to choose our actions and live our lives in any manner that pleases us. However, though we are at liberty to do as we please, we can avoid the consequences of our life choices. We can choose to surrender and follow God's path or take another road. But know that taking any path separated from the guiding and protective will of God will lead to pain and destruction. My past turmoil is now my testimony.

Akilah

My husband and I met in college and began dating freshman year. In fact, we were married just one year after graduation. Babes, I tell you, merely babes! I had been raised by a single mom in the not-so-great part of town. She taught me that education and exposure to things that would give me a greater fervor for the better things in life were the keys to obtaining them. I heeded my mother's advice, and with a focus on education and a very independent spirit, I set out as an adult in the world. Since my now husband and I went through our college years together, fell madly in love, and vowed to commit to each other for the rest of our lives, we really did grow up together, figuring it all out as we went. /surrender)

As Tyrone mentioned earlier, he came to know Christ in his young-adult years, but I had always attended church, grew up in the church, you know one of the "been in church all my life" saints. Yup, that's me, except I was the "in church every night of the week; choir director's kid; deacon, deaconess, and trustee's granddaughter" kind of "grew up in church" person. So, when T. Jay (as I affectionately call him) and I began dating, church was a must. It's easy to guess that even once we began our family, continuing to go to church was a no-brainer. We went to Sunday service faithfully. Our kids were in Sunday school learning about

Jesus, and we were getting the Word in the main sanctuary. In fact, one Sunday when our daughter was around five, both she and T. Jay weren't feeling so well as time approached for us to head out to weekly service. We decided to stay home, and our daughter's response was, "That's okay, we can just have church here." This five-year old proceeded to sing a Jesus song, encouraging us to join in, of course, had us tell a Bible story to her and her brother, and even came up with a design of a suitable craft—a paper "Gospel CD" fully decorated with crosses which she kept on her bedroom door knob for about a year after, by the way. So yeah, we knew Christ and were walking the right path, so we thought. But God wanted more from us.

Surrender and submission go hand in hand. In order to surrender yourself, you have to submit to another's authority. Spoiler alert—this wasn't an easy task for me. Being raised to be independent, I took that same attitude into my marriage. As my husband and I started a family and I became the primary caregiver for our children as a stay-at-home mom, I fell into stride with managing our home. I oversaw the kid's education, set all of our schedules, determined how much money we had to do the things we wanted to do and when we'd do them. T. Jay was the CEO, but I was the COO of the Jefferson Estate.

As my husband said, coming out of the "great credit debacle of 2006," we'd really ramped up our faith-walk. We began attending our church's Bible study and marriage ministry events, taking classes to improve ourselves, and even serving in ministry. One such class was a wives class where the dirty word was mentioned. You know the one. The "S" word. Submission. It was quite intriguing to see these women, otherwise strong and opinionated, shrink down when the facilitator raised the question, "Are you submitting to God through the vessel He sent as an authority figure in your life, your husband?"

> *"Wives, likewise, be submissive to your own husbands, that even if some do not obey the word, they, without a word, may be won by the conduct of their wives."*
>
> *1 Peter 3:1*

Despite having grown up in a Baptist church, the idea of submission was very new to me. My thoughts on the matter were: "So, I am supposed to ask my husband what he thinks about the plans I have created for our family or, better yet, ask him for his plans, consider his thoughts, and follow his lead? Even if his conclusion doesn't match my logical one? Really? And this is what God wants from me, this is how I surrender and submit? Okay, I'll try it, but how will I show that I've done that?" And as He always does, God showed me the way.

> *"Trust in the LORD with all your heart and lean not on your own understanding; in all your ways submit to him, and he will make your paths straight."*
>
> *Proverbs 3:5-6*

Hurricane Irene came and graced our lovely state in 2011. The category 1 hurricane packed sustained winds nearing 85 mph. In our area, it was recorded that between 5-11 inches of rain fell within a 24-hour period. The basement in the Jefferson Estate flooded and flooded badly! We'd not had any issues with water intruding our home before, so we were not prepared. The days, weeks, and couple of months that followed found us all living on one level in our home, with all of our belongings from both levels crowded around us. We were safe, however, and had minimal damage to our things. We developed a plan, the insurance adjuster came and deemed that we would get the funds to repair, and after it was all said and done, this trial would end in triumph because I was getting a remodeled basement. Oh yeah! Or so I thought.

As life would have it, when demo began, asbestos was found. Not only a time setback but a huge financial hit, as all of the money that was going to my pretty new flooring and updated furniture was no more. But T. Jay, determined to make the best out of the situation, put on his weekend warrior armor and together with a family member rebuilt our basement. Now, it wasn't furnished, but it was functional, as family member donations pieced it together just fine.

There was this one area where we...I...we...okay...I wanted a bistro table and accompanying chairs. I thought it would be the perfect place to do family game night and school projects with the kids and serve as a nice, entertaining space when family and friends visited. I set out to find the right deal because being a single-income household, having a deal was a must. I visited furniture stores and outlets alike looking for the perfectly-sized right-priced piece. And then it happened. I found one and at my favorite concentric red circle store nonetheless! This was perfect, the price was right, but they were selling out fast. Wanna know how I knew? Because I called several stores to ensure they had it before driving to any of them (another money-saving technique I had garnered under my belt). But boom, I had found one in a neighboring state, not far away, and they were holding it for me. My plan was to scoot across the bridge and scoop it up that evening.

As I set out to get my perfect table, I gave my husband a courtesy call telling him where I was headed, that I'd be late getting home, and that I would need help unloading it when I arrived. You know, I was doing the "submission" thing. Okay, fine, it was still the "me in control pretending to be submitted" thing, but hey, I was trying, right? I wasn't able to reach him when I called, but hey, I tried, and we'd discussed earlier in the day that I'd be purchasing the table, so I headed in the opposite direction of home toward the store. I got a return call just as I was taking the on-ramp for the highway. The conversation didn't quite go as I thought it would. T. Jay, my husband, the man I love dearly, the one for which I had born and lovingly cared for his two children said to me, "I don't think we need the table; just come home." I was thoroughly confused. We'd discussed this, agreed on this, the price was right, they had it on hold, and I was already driving in the direction of the store. He reiterated his point that we didn't need it, even though the space we'd identified for it sat empty even as we spoke (Can you hear the disdain I had for his decision?). I argued my point, quick and concise, expressing my opposition. In the end, he relented and said these words, "Do what you want." I had won, or so I figured, so I continued on my way.

The Holy Spirit spoke to me in that exact moment. I heard a voice clearly say, "Turn around." I responded just as quickly, "But he said do what I want, so he co-signed the purchase." The Holy Spirit said to me a second time, "Turn around." I breathed a heavy sigh of defeat, "Really God? Okay fine," and took the last exit on my side of the state line to head home. Now, this exit has some really long on and off-ramps, a very convoluted merging of several highways, so I had the time to "think on things" as I was changing directions. I inserted myself again, thinking, "You know what, I have been waiting for this table for quite some time. We have endured so many things just trying to get our house in order. God wants the best for us, and T. Jay did say do I what I want, so he's in agreement with me. I'm going to get my table." Did you see "*my*"? Instead of now taking the ramp to head home, I chose to get back on the highway headed back toward the store. I had squared up my shoulders, checked the time to make sure I could get there before the store closed, and settled in myself that I was coming home with this table. I was on the bridge that connects the two states, and the Holy Spirit said to me a third time, "Turn around." Now with defeat and anger in my heart, I took the next exit (it was also the way to the store), but I turned around one last time. I crossed the bridge again and headed home. When I pulled into our driveway and got out of the car, T. Jay was waiting for me, anticipating carrying the table into the house. He greeted me and said, "That was quick; where's the table?" My exact words to him were, "It's not submission if I agree," and I stormed past him into the house.

Later on that night, I prayed about the situation. I asked God to forgive me for my attitude and to please give me a heart of repentance and change me. I had been so strong-willed that I was allowing, better yet welcoming, drama into our home. A change needed to happen, and I was the one who needed to do it. That night, I committed to being submitted to my husband. I realized that I had not been truly submitted to God if I couldn't be submitted to my husband. I had to surrender—surrender my thoughts, my ideas, my ideals, my will to God.

> *"I beseech you therefore, brethren, by the mercies of God, that you present your bodies a living sacrifice, holy, acceptable to God, which is your reasonable service. And do not be conformed to this world, but be transformed by the renewing of your mind, that you may prove what is that good and acceptable and perfect will of God."*
>
> *Romans 12:1-2*

While this wasn't an overnight process walking in submission, I do believe that God saw my commitment to having a heart change. And just as our "good, good Father" does, He blessed me.

Two days after my table drama ordeal, I got a phone call from a relative. This relative worked in a high-end retail store, and the company was doing a total design overhaul of the store. Everything that was not merchandise had to go as they were bringing in brand-new fixtures for the entire store. My relative asked me about a specific piece, a round table that they'd used to fold clothes. She told me that it was free, all I needed to do was pick it up. I sat on the other end of the phone in disbelief. Free? Free! Could God really be rewarding me for my heart change? Could He really think enough of *me* to do this for me, even with the way I had acted? I called T. Jay and asked if we could accept the table, and when he agreed, I was overjoyed. We got the table into place, and even though it was not what I had originally chosen, it fit the space even better; it was perfect for our needs. I knew that not only making the commitment to do things God's way was the right thing to do but also that God had shown me in a real-life, everyday-kind-of-way circumstance how I could surrender and submit to Him.

> *"My son, give me your heart and let your eyes delight in my ways."*
> *Proverbs 23:26*

Now, can I tell you that surrender is so freeing? I don't have to carry the weight of the outcome. Don't get me wrong, I do have to be responsible in my decisions, but I know God has me covered. I just turn over situations to Him and ask that He guide my path, and I follow.

We've all seen at the end of a battle when it's clear who the victor is and the losing side raises and waves the little white flag of defeat. I submit to you that in our lives as Christians, we have to acknowledge that we're already the victors because we're on the winning team with Christ. So, when you're in the seasons of despair, facing the hard decisions of the world, raise your little white flag but not in defeat. Instead, raise it in surrender. Surrender to God, and His peace, His joy, will be granted to you.

> *"Call upon Me in the day of trouble; I will deliver you, and you shall glorify Me."*
> *Psalms 50:15*

iHOPE

*"The Lord takes pleasure in those who fear Him,
in those who hope in His mercy."*
(Psalm 147:11 NKJV)

Contributions by: Corey and Shaunda Bellamy

In order to be a successful Christian, I believe that hope, faith, and the fear of God need to be interwoven in the heart of every believer. Hebrews 11:1 tells us, *"Faith is the substance of things hoped for, the evidence of things not seen."* In the past, I read this text with a focus on defining faith while overlooking hope. I now see that the writer of Hebrews was conveying to us that faith is birthed out of our unseen expectations of what we desire from God. Hope then represents our internalized expectations, while faith is the outward expression of the same. Therefore, without hope, faith is impossible. Hope is defined in many ways, but the definition that stands out to me is "a feeling of desire for something and confidence in the possibility of its fulfillment." (True Gift, 2013)

The piece that I will add is that our confidence is in God. For with God, all things are possible.

Hope is not only a key element needed for every sincere Christian, but hope is also a key ingredient needed for every successful marriage. When I look back over the life of our relationship, including our marriage, I can clearly see characteristics of hope in many situations and circumstances that we have experienced. As you journey with us through a few accounts of challenging situations that we've experienced, it is our hope that you will be able to see the same characteristics of hope throughout and that our hope in God ignites the same for you.

THE BEGINNING

The summer before my senior year in high school, I saw my wife riding a bicycle through the parking lot of Sandy Ridge Apartments, and I began to tell my little cousin all the good things that I knew about her. At the time, I only knew her from a distance, but I was confident that I would get to know her better eventually. I told my cousin at that time that Shaunda would be my wife. My actual words were, "I'm going to marry her." As I think back on that time, I am not sure why I was so confident about marrying her but it was like I just knew it. We had met earlier in high school. Although we attended different schools, Shaunda's aunt and my mother worked together at a local non-profit organization, and we volunteered together a few times. We became friends and eventually began dating late during our senior year of high school. There are many who like to take the credit for "hooking us up," but we both know that God ultimately gets the credit for bringing us together.

I remember as graduation was approaching, I told Corey that I thought we should not be together when we went to college because we were going to different schools. I really wanted to remain friends with him, and I did not want anything to jeopardize the friendship we had created. Well, of course that did not happen, and we remained together throughout college. After college, I decided to move to the DMV. As an accountant, I felt that I would have great opportunities here in the DC Metropolitan area. Corey soon followed (smile). We both rededicated our lives to God and joined First Baptist of Glenarden (FBCG). I lived in Alexandria, VA, and he lived in Upper Marlboro, MD, but it was something about FBCG that changed our lives. We began to serve in the church, and we also began to gain a better understanding of God's love for us. It is my belief that the teachings of FBCG really taught us to better love ourselves and to better love one another.

After Corey completed his master's degree, he proposed to me, and I said, "Yes." It was my birthday, and we were in Jamaica for a wedding. His proposal was so thoughtful. Early one morning, Corey began to read 1 Corinthians 13:4-8, *"Love suffers long and is kind; love does not envy; love does not parade itself, is not puffed up; does not behave rudely, does not seek its own, is not provoked, thinks no evil; does not rejoice in iniquity, but rejoices in the truth; bears all things, believes all things, hopes all things, endures all things. Love never fails."* Once he finished reading the scripture, he asked me to marry him. He did not actually have a ring, but he had a picture of the ring he said he would buy for me. After I said yes, he pulled out the real ring and placed it on my finger. I did not realize it at the time, but 1 Corinthians 13:4-8 would be one of the foundational scriptures of our marriage. Soon after we got married, our vows would be tested—for better, for worse, in sickness, and in health.

The Test – Part 1

A few months after we were married, I became ill. I was having health issues before we got married, but it got worse as time progressed. I lost so much weight. I went from a size six down to a size two. For several months, we dealt with the changes that my body was going through. We were newlyweds and already facing challenges due to illness. Illness can put a strain on marriage at any stage, but imagine how difficult it can be for newlyweds. We were just coming together as one, adjusting to living with and really learning about one another. Studies show that marriages in which one spouse has a chronic illness are more likely to fail if the spouses are young (WebMD, 2012). We were a young couple at the time, but we had an expectation that God would turn things around for us. It was really difficult to deal with, but we remained faithful and trusted God for complete and total healing. During the time that we were dealing with this, I remembered that 1 Corinthians 13:4-8 was the foundational scripture for our marriage and that scripture was one of the scriptures that helped navigate us through this particular challenge. Finally, after about one year, the doctors were able to prescribe some medication that calmed the symptoms down. I was doing much better, and things were considered normal. I felt like we could finally be what I viewed as newlyweds, without the strain of sickness.

The Test – Part 2

About a year after we got through our first health challenge, I began to feel some slight pain in my right knee. Right after I graduated from college, I had noticed slight stiffness in my right knee each year when the weather changed from hot to cold. I never tried to figure out why I experienced the stiffness because it did not inhibit me from completing daily tasks. Now, about two years into our marriage, what had started out as slight knee pain and stiffness progressed to an annoying knee pain. I continued on until the pain was unbearable, and in 2007, I was no longer able to walk on my right knee. We began seeing different physicians who were prescribing a variety of different medications that did not work, and none of the physicians could offer a proper diagnosis. Meanwhile, the pain became so unbearable that I could not even sleep through the night. This time, Corey moved into the role of a caregiver for me. I remember waking up one night and hearing Corey praying for me in the living room. He was praying for God to relieve my pain. At first, I thought I was dreaming, but I began to hear him clearly. I distinctly remember feeling sad for Corey at that moment. I know that we took the vows for better or worse, but it felt as if we had not really experienced better yet. We finally connected with a physician who diagnosed me with an autoimmune illness. After physical therapy, autoimmune suppressants, etc., I was doing a lot better—just a new normal. One medication that I was prescribed caused birth defects. Therefore, we were advised not to get pregnant because of the potential damage the medication would cause for our unborn child. This truly grieved me because I knew how much Corey loved and wanted children. We fasted and prayed for a child, and we did not focus on what the doctor had said. We knew that I would need to stop taking the medication in order to conceive. I began to have dreams about a little girl, my little girl. I remember writing the name Zoe on a piece of paper and sticking it in the Bible in 1 Samuel Chapter 1. First Samuel is the story of Elkanah and his two wives, Hannah and Peninnah. Peninnah had children; however, Hannah had not been able to conceive. In this scripture, Hannah prayed to God to open up her womb, and God did honor her prayer. I believed God for Zoe, so I began to pray Hannah's prayer. Finally, in the fall of 2015, my doctor gave me a break in taking the medication that caused birth defects because my health had significantly improved. Early in 2016, we found out that we were pregnant. You can imagine how excited we were because this was what we had prayed and fasted for. Immediately, I began speaking over baby Zoe (which means life). It was definitely too early for us to choose a name as we did not even know the gender yet. As we began going to my appointments, we noticed that my HCG levels (the pregnancy hormones) were not doubling as they should have. Instead, my levels were only incrementally increasing. The doctor told us that she did not think the baby would survive, and she encouraged us to abort our baby. Instead of following the advice of the doctor, we held on to Hebrews 10:23, *"Let us hold fast the confession of our hope without wavering, for He who promised is faithful."* We had received a prophecy that we would conceive, that it would be a beautiful, intelligent daughter. Our hope was in God and not what the doctor was saying to us. We continued praying and believing God for life. One day when I was sitting at work, I started having the worst abdominal pain that I have ever experienced, and I also had some bleeding. I rushed to the emergency room. After being examined, I was told that I was at the beginning stage of having a miscarriage. They sent me home and of course, we continued to pray. I finally fell asleep, and I woke up in excruciating pain. I cried and prayed until I fell asleep again. While I was sleeping, I dreamed that I was holding my friend Tamika's hand. She had passed away the year prior, it was as if she was trying to be there for me like she had been so many times before. The pain finally woke me up out of my sleep, and I was actually having the miscarriage. I was devasted because we had prayed and fasted for this child. We know that God is not a God who would lie; He would not honor our request to get pregnant and then allow us to lose the baby that He gave us. I began to meditate on God and not on the miscarriage, and it was clear to me that God was doing something through the miscarriage. The scripture James 1:2-4 came to mind, which states, *"My brethren, count it all joy when you fall into various trials, knowing that the testing of your faith produces patience. But let patience have its perfect work, that you may be perfect and complete, lacking nothing."* In other words, we should rejoice in our suffering because our suffering produces perseverance, perseverance produces character, and character produces hope.

Over the next few months, it was definitely a character-building period for us. I grieved the loss, and I could not understand how I could be so hurt over someone I never actually saw. I had experienced so much loss that it all seemed to be coming down on me at one time. I began to think of my dear friend Tamika. I began thinking about the little things about our friendship that we sometimes took for granted. We shared our ups and downs, rejoicing with one another over triumphs and crying with one another over our failures and disappointments. At that point, I realized that I had been suppressing grief over the loss of my sister friend. It was a feeling like nothing I had ever experienced at the time. Several of my loved ones had passed, from my grandparents, aunts, uncles, cousins, and friends. During each loss, Tamika was right there with me. Now, at one of the most painful times in my life, I did not have my sister friend to share my deepest thoughts with. Of course,

I had Corey, who also shared in my grief. However, Tamika and I were the last of our crew who had not conceived. In my mind, she would have known exactly what I was experiencing at this age and stage of my life. It was complicated grief. Corey convinced me to take some time to just process my emotions.

The Test – Part 3

Soon after the miscarriage, I returned to work, and it was business as usual. I began to lose what little weight I had gained during pregnancy. After losing the weight from pregnancy, one day I noticed that I could feel a small lump in my right breast. I told Corey about it, and we decided that I would call my Ob-gyn. I called my Ob-gyn and explained to her what I was feeling. She explained to me that during pregnancy your breasts change, and she assured me that I had nothing to worry about. She also told me I was too young for breast cancer. I accepted what the Ob-gyn said. However, as I lost more weight, the lump seemed to feel harder and more pronounced. I called my Ob-gyn on two more occasions to be told the same thing. I became frustrated with her because she had not examined me, and I did not understand how she could make a decision that what I was feeling was nothing to worry about without seeing for herself. I decided to contact my primary care physician. After receiving a mammogram, sonogram, and biopsy, I was diagnosed with stage 3 Her-2 estrogen positive ductal carcinoma breast cancer. As I sat listening to the diagnosis from the breast surgeon, I just felt shocked. My thoughts immediately went to Corey and how we had already walked through so much. However, one thing I did know was that we both had faith. At this point, we had to have unshakable faith. Unshakable faith is faith that can endure whatever comes into your path. We all need this type of faith because life can sometimes shake our faith. With unshakable faith, we can handle whatever circumstances God permits in our lives, understanding that as children of God, if He permits it, He will protect you. I refocused and listened to the surgeon while she explained that if I had gone full term with the pregnancy, I may not have made it. The form of cancer that I was diagnosed with thrived off hormones, and it is considered aggressive in women who are in childbearing years. During pregnancy, in trying to produce milk, the tumor was pushed to the surface of my breast so that I could feel it. The tumor was there before the pregnancy, but it was not noticeable at all. My thought at the time was that God had used the tragedy of my miscarriage to save my life. Zoe, which means life, gave me life. The heavy grief of the miscarriage left me, and I was now focused on beating cancer.

We learned the lesson that although we may pray specific prayers, God's answer to those prayers may be no or not now. When the answer is no, we should do as the Scriptures tell us and *"lean not to our own understanding, and in all thine ways, acknowledge Him."* (Proverbs 3:5-6) The "No" could save your life. Romans 8:28 reads, *"And we know that all things work together for good to those who love God, to those who are the called according to His purpose."* Because we knew that God exposed it, we were confident that He would heal me.

The next year was truly a test of our faith, our hope, and our love for each other. Through mental and physical changes, Corey still told me that I was beautiful. Corey was serving as my caregiver and running his business at the same time. The first six months of treatment were like going to work. We were at the hospital from six to eight hours, depending on what was taking place on that particular day. Corey never missed a chemotherapy appointment, even when others offered to step in to go with me. He kindly said, "No, thank you." We were in warrior mode. During treatment, it felt as if everything else we had experienced since we had gotten married was practice for this moment. Instead of this difficult time breaking us apart, it made us cling closer together. After about two months of treatment, I began fainting a day or two after each treatment. The doctors ran various tests to determine the cause of these fainting spells. It was determined that I was experiencing heart failure as a side effect of one of the chemotherapy drugs. We were told that my heart might never return to normal functioning. We prayed and continued believing God for my healing. After I completed surgery and my treatment and was cancer-free, I went to my annual checkup with the cardiologist, and she informed me that my heart was operating at a function higher than before I began treatment. We held on to God's promises, and we experienced the meaning of Ecclesiastes 4:9-12. Ecclesiastes 4:9-12 states:

> *Two are better than one, because they have a good reward for their labor. For if they fall, one will lift up his companion. But woe to him who is alone when he falls, for he has no one to help him up. Again, if two lie down together, they will keep warm; But how can one be warm alone? Though one may be overpowered by another, two can withstand him. And a threefold cord is not quickly broken.*

LESSONS LEARNED

As a husband, each of the situations that Shaunda has written about made me stronger. It taught me how to lean and depend completely on God for my strength. Through each challenge, I was able to grow closer to God and closer to Shaunda. My parents have been married for over fifty years, and although I did not see it growing up, I know they had many challenges. I often use my father as a source of inspiration for accomplishing anything that I set out to accomplish, and having a successful marriage is no different. My father has inspired me to be a great husband and to have a great marriage. I entered into this covenant with Shaunda with expectations of nothing less than a successful marriage. Through each test, I knew that it was my responsibility as her husband to be by her side offering prayer, encouragement, and support. Test 1 was a true challenge, but I remembered how she took care of me as my girlfriend when I experienced a serious illness. I knew that if she was that committed as my girlfriend, that she would be even more caring and committed as my wife. Test 2 was devastating to me. We were really excited about bringing a life into this world, and our pregnancy was an answered prayer. When it ended in a miscarriage, I was hurt, but I still have an expectation that God will do it for us again.

While the first two situations were very difficult, breast cancer was scary. We were actually still dealing with the grief of the miscarriage when we were hit with cancer. Although I tried not to show it, I was devastated by that news. It took me a day or two to completely pull myself together. I prayed for strength, and God gave it to me. I had no clue what we were up against, but God saw us through. I consider myself a fixer, and I try to fix everything. During cancer treatment, I could not fix it. I had to watch Shaunda suffer through it. Some days, I would just stare at her, wishing I could take the pain away. I felt that I could have handled it better if I was the one suffering the pain. I suffered more by having to watch her suffer, but I knew that I had to be strong for her and to do everything in my power to help her during this period.

Having a loving companion to walk through the most difficult times of life is a blessing. With commitment and patience, we have learned to handle the tension and stress that multiple illnesses have placed on our marriage. We placed our hope in God through every situation that we have faced. The world would have you believe that when young marriages are faced with illness of one spouse, the marriage will fail. However, with God at the center of our marriage, we have seen how facing illness has helped us form a closer bond. Even at this time in our marriage, we have faith in God that we will conceive. Hebrews 11:11, *"By faith Sarah herself also received strength to conceive seed, and she bore a child when she was past the age, because she judged Him faithful who had promised."* During this phase of our marriage, we are seeking God to clearly hear from Him, and we are excited about what He has in store for us. To God be the glory for the things that He has done!

iTRUST

Trust in the Lord with all your heart, and lean not on your own understanding; In all your ways acknowledge Him, And He shall direct your paths.
(Proverbs 3:5-6 NKJV)
Contributions by: Anthony and Lisa Jones

This is a scripture that we have heard, recited, and learned of its meaning from our elders yet did not understand its implication in our lives until we were married. We had the pleasure of beginning our lives as one over twenty-four years ago—a day filled with love, laughs, hopes, and dreams. A day celebrated with us by our family and friends, yet what do you do when life and reality come at you full fledge?

IN THE BEGINNING

We trusted that God would make a way. We were married, had a baby by year two, were gainfully employed, bought the house and cars. Life was good, so trusting God at this point was easy.

We were able to take strolls in the park and on the beach either as a couple or as a family. We worshiped together on Sunday morning. We ministered to others through song as members of the choir.

So, what do you do when one of you loses their job, the mortgage is due, daycare payment is due, and food needs to be in the house? How do you remain encouraged when all feels lost? We can tell you, we TRUSTED GOD and prayed.

During a period of unemployment, as we prayed together and cried out to God for His covering and help, we went to the mailbox to see an unexpected check show up so we could buy milk and Pampers for the baby. We had family members bless us with gifts that kept us afloat. We knew that the only way that this was possible was the intervening power of God.

THROUGH THE YEARS

As a couple, we have been faced with the challenges of life that were designed to test our faith and make us question our purpose. During these times, we have learned to TRUST the process that we couldn't see, a true testament to our FAITH. At times, we failed the test. We argued and refused to speak to each other. We went to bed night after night, ignoring the fact that one or both of us could have slipped away into the great beyond, yet God loved us enough to spare our lives to try again.

We have faced trials and tribulations that forced the two of us who have cleaved as one to address traumas in our lives that wanted to shield us from our destiny. We combated issues that included abandonment, anxiety, depression, and PTSD, just to name a few. As a couple, we sought the services of a clinical psychologist who assisted us with working through the baggage that we had brought into the marriage and needed to work through so that our marriage would make it through, regardless of what the devil wanted. We also realized that if God allowed it to happen to us, then there was a greater purpose for us.

With that being said, we also participated in an exercise that made our hearts hurt; however, it opened our eyes to really understand that we are not to take life for granted. As part of an exercise for our counseling session, we had to answer a writing prompt that stated, "Write a letter to your spouse who is on their deathbed; what would you say with these last moments left?"

Anthony Wrote:

To my love, Lisa. Forgive me for all of the challenges that we endured as a couple, especially the ones that I caused. I always wanted the best for you and the children and at times went about it the wrong way. I appreciate you loving me through the good and the bad, in sickness and in health, until death. Continue to carry our love in your heart. I will always be watching over you. Until we meet again, your husband. --Anthony

Lisa Wrote:

My dearest Anthony. I love you. I apologize for the many times that I let life happen without focusing on us. I am sorry for the arguments that had no meaning yet wasted our precious time on foolishness. Now, as I gain the strength to say...until we meet again, just know that I love you. You have been my friend, lover, and father to our children. I never wanted to imagine life without you. I love you now and forever. I love you for my soul. Forever in my heart. --Lisa

Having had this experience, we committed to work through the stressors of life. We realized that it would be hard, and we were willing to try. We embraced our church's motto for marriage— divorce is not an option, unless domestic violence is involved.

OUR CURRENT SITUATION

We our leaning not on what we see or hear. We are trusting in God to continue to order our steps. We seek God in our decision-making and wait for Him to give us an answer. At times, it's not in our anticipated time that we want to hear; however, I can truly tell you—the response is always on time.

Our lessons learned along with the biblical principles of our church have us involved in facilitating classes for other married couples to stay the course and study together to understand God's design and hope for marriages.

WHAT ARE WE WITNESSING?

To intentionally interact daily with my spouse
Respect the process; God's design for marriage is written in the Bible, and we need to read and study it accordingly in order to reach its benefits.

Understand that somethings will not come soon. It requires patience.

Support each other, regardless of the struggle.

Take time for each other. Our first ministry is to one another.

We had another exercise that resonated with us as a couple through our experiences in our church class. We had to share what we've learned and gained from the marriage class. Our final exercise included our view of the state of the marriage.

In our writing about the state of the marriage, we both wrote our narrative independently and shared it with each other once we were together with our facilitators. What we found was that we both shared similar themes in our responses.

OUR SUMMATION

Our marriage before beginning the class, we were having ups and downs and wondering what the next steps should be for the marriage. We were participating in marriage counseling with a clinical marriage counselor, who was assisting us with working through the issues that were tearing our marriage apart. Yet, there were still areas of growth that were still needed in our marriage. In other words, my spouse and I were not on the same page with moving forward. There was a selfishness there that focused on one-sidedness, the "I" and not "we."

We knew our love language; however, if it wasn't being displayed by both parties, then no one received any kind of implementation. For example, one spouse's love language is affirmation, and the other's is physical touch. If the spouse didn't feel affirmed, then there wasn't any attempt to speak to the love language of physical touch. Truthfully, we were in a place of paying for a marriage counselor in hope that we would get to the root of the problem(s) so that we could determine our next steps, would that next step be to seek a legal separation so that we could co-parent and not continue our current path of not fulfilling each other in the marriage.

The truth is that we loved each other; however, we had become exhausted with trying to understand and meet each other's needs. We didn't want a divorce; however, we wanted a peace of mind to be healthy and happy emotionally, spiritually, and physically.

Currently, we are attempting to implement the strategies taught within the text we read along with the tools that we have gained from the class. The goal is to become more consistent with using the tools so that our marriage will improve. We do, however, believe that we currently have a positive outlook for our marriage.

The goals that we have for our marriage are as follows:

- Continuing to implement prayer in our marriage daily, individually and collectively.
- Keeping God at the center.
- Consistently having devotion with one another for the improvement of the marriage.
- Setting up time that we minister to the needs of each other before we meet the needs of others.

In order to arrive at these goals, we must continue to seek God first in everything and refrain from looking at our spouse. We must look at ourselves and our actions and always reflect on this question,

"Would God be happy with me with this decision that I am making in my marriage?"

With this being said, we were continually taught the lesson TRUST in the GOD and the process of marriage and have FAITH that if God allowed it to happen, it's for our good and we have to be obedient. We have to die to self in order to fulfill the promises of God for our marriage.

Often times, we reflect on a message that Anthony delivered. The tag line that resonates with us is:

> *God works in you before he works through you…you were made for ministry!*

Our marriage is a ministry, our very first ministry. We must operate with open eyes to what God wants for marriage. We do not want to operate our lives being disobedient to God's plan. In the book of Titus 3: 3-8, it says:

Once we, too, were foolish and disobedient. We were misled and became slaves to many lusts and pleasures. Our lives were full of evil and envy, and we hated each other. But when God our Savior revealed his kindness and love, he saved us, not because of the righteous things we had done, but because of his mercy. He washed away our sins, giving us a new birth and new life through the Holy Spirit. He generously poured out the Spirit upon us through Jesus Christ our Savior. Because of his grace he made us right in his sight and gave us confidence that we will inherit eternal life. This is a trustworthy saying, and I want you to insist on these teachings so that all who trust in God will devote themselves to doing good. These teachings are good and beneficial for everyone.

Paul summarized here that following a life of pleasure and giving into every sensual desire leads to slavery. **<u>Christ does for us what we could not do for ourselves when He saved us!</u>** (Dr. Love, Survey of Christian Doctrine I & II at Bethel Seminary). We have no choice but to move from a life full of sin to one where we are led by the Holy Spirit when we surrender our will to the will of God. We must exercise our faith.

In the New Testament, Paul clarified that God's grace saves us through faith. God gives us grace, His unmerited favor. We respond to this gift by exercising our faith! Ultimately, God saves us; we don't save ourselves! Let us say that again—**we don't and can't save ourselves from the consequences of our sin!** If we choose not to follow what God says when He tells us to operate within our marriage, then why do we expect our marriage to flourish? We have to exercise our faith that God will do what He always tells us He will do in His Book. We have to exercise our faith in Jesus.

It's just like when you start a new exercise regimen in order to get your body in shape and live a healthier lifestyle, (you know how you all have the gym memberships at LA Fitness, Gold's Gym, Planet Fitness that you don't use for whatever reason) but in order to achieve your goal of a healthier lifestyle, you have to put forth some real and concerted effort. You have to eat right and work out daily, and eventually, over a period of time and after some hard work, you will have that physical appearance that is attractive to others (and yourself). You're working real hard at trying to please man. Well, I submit to you, if you put forth that same concerted level of effort, I know a coach, a personal trainer, who can guarantee you will have a healthier life and will live with Him forever in paradise. It is going to require you to **exercise your faith; you must** believe that the Lord Jesus Christ died on the cross for your sins, was buried (went to hell for three days, conquered death, and got the keys), and rose from the dead so that you and I might have access to LIFE—then you too can have a **new body, a renewed healthier life with Jesus Christ, and your marriage will represent Christ and His love of the church!** So, why don't you **WORK YOUR FAITH? Step out and risk believing in Jesus! We know you might not have all or any of the answers, but trust God! It's as simple as "ABC!" "A" – admit we have sinned and fallen short of God's glory. "B" – believe that Jesus died for our sins on the cross. And "C" – Commit your life to Jesus as Lord and Savior. We surrender to you, Jesus; take control! Become our Master! Rule and reign over our lives! Guide and protect our marriage. It's Your will and not ours!**

Let us share what we mean by this term **"faith"** for which we are continuously referencing. We see from Hebrews 11:1 that *"Faith is the substance of things hoped for, the evidence of things not seen;"* this **faith** is the connecting power into the spiritual realm, which links us with God and makes Him become a tangible reality to the natural perception of man. It is the basic ingredient to begin a relationship with God. In the *Greek,* we get its root from the feminine noun *PISTIS*— which means credence, assurance, belief, moral conviction, and faith; and in the *Hebrew* from of the word, the feminine noun *AMANAH* is translated as a covenant or firm foundation/portion. So, with that: (1) *It is impossible to be saved without faith, and without faith, it is impossible to please God. (2) Everything in salvation is based on faith. We must believe in that which we cannot see. It is that faith which is a spiritual force that overcomes great opposition and can carry a person through great trials* *and triumphs over circumstances in the natural realm.* It is that faith for which Abraham is known, as he believed God's promise to give him and his barren wife a son. So, why then, would God now test Abraham with his marriage for the very thing that He promised with the unthinkable and unimaginable act of sacrificing his [Abraham, that is] only begotten son? **See, you missed it. It went right over your head. I need you all to catch that parallel right there!** I can't imagine how Abraham must have felt when God sent this test!

So, let us take a deeper look at the scripture—in verse 1, it reads, *"Now it came to pass after these things that God tested Abraham."* So, here is my question for us to consider: **"Why did God have to test Abraham?"** God wasn't trying to trip up Abraham or deliberately see him fall. But I believe that He [God] wanted to deepen Abraham's capacity to obey God and as a result, develop his character within his marriage. A point or theme that we would like for you to ponder—**"Can God trust you?"**

We are never secure from trials, especially in our marriage. Every trial is indeed a temptation that tends to show the real dispositions of the heart, whether holy or unholy. Can God trust that when you are faced with strong, vigorous, and seemingly relentless trials and tribulation that you will not draw unto a sinful manner in which to deal with your current circumstance? Just as the fire refines the ore to extract the precious metal, God refines us through difficult circumstances in order that we might become more like Him.

Observe this with us here if you would that it says, *"...it came to pass after these things;"* logically, it would appear that after all the difficulties you have gone through to get to this place, that now perhaps the storms of life have settled and you would be good. But instead, you are faced with the biggest encounter/challenge of your life! Really, God? I'm expecting You to ratify a promise, but instead, You are asking me that after it has come to pass to now sacrifice the greatest gift You have given to me. We can choose to complain about the test, or we can try to see how God is stretching us to develop our character. **Can God trust you?**

Let's look at what God is asking to be offered. In verse 2, it says, *"Take now your son, your only son Isaac, whom you love, and go to the land of Moriah, and offer him there as a burnt offering on one of the mountains of which I shall tell you."* Now how many of you after all you had to go through to have a child, not just any child, but your only son, that if God told you to go and kill your only child would not only be hesitant but might ask God, "**Whatchu talking about Willis?**" No, seriously though, all things considered—would you not have issue with that command? God, You gave me a promise, and now You are asking me to give You a sacrifice. Which brings us to our next point, "**Where is your faith?**"

In 1985, Malaco Records released a live recording at Pisgah Baptist Church by the late Rev. James Cleveland titled, **"Where is your faith?"** In the **original lyrics** of that song, the verse says:

Faith is the substance of things hoped for, the evidence of things not seen. Faith will keep you when your way seems dark; (faith, faith, where is your faith in God)?

Christians, you say that you love the Lord, and yet we complain each day seems hard. Into each life some rain must fall; (faith, faith, where is your faith in God)?

The chorus goes on to say:

> *Faith can move mountains,*
> *Faith can open the fountain,*
> *Oh, faith can help you succeed,*
> *Oh, faith can supply your every need;*

> *Where is your faith in God?*

But somewhere between the writing of the original lyrics and the actual live recording, God must have asked the reverend a few questions about his faith. We can only imagine what those questions must have been because in the recording, Rev. Cleveland tells us the story of two Christians who were talking; one was a backslider, who was complaining that everything was going wrong for him and that God must not love him, so the Christian was trying to encourage him and thus we got these lyrics:

> *Said you've been sick...you don't think you can make it...*
> *tell me about it. Where is your faith?*

> *Said you're in trouble...tell me about it. Got to go to court next week...*
> *where is your faith?*

> *Say you are out of work...tell me about it...my money ran out and all*
> *my bills are way past due...where is your faith?*

We can only imagine that when God said to Abraham to his great amazement, *"Go kill your son,"* that this command given him in such aggravating language would have grievously tempted Abraham to disobey God; but Abraham, no doubt, took notice of every word and listened attentively to it, and every word there was like a sword in his bones—God was sublimely asking Abraham, ***"Where is your faith?"*** Observe with us here the person to be offered. "Take now your son, your only son"—God didn't ask for his bullocks and lambs; oh, we can only imagine how willingly Abraham would have parted with them, by the thousands no less to redeem his son Isaac!

In God's command to Abraham for him to sacrifice his only son whom he loved so dearly and was given to him and Sarah as a promise was a test of Abraham's love toward God and he and his wife's obedience. **See, we came back to it so you would catch it.** You know what the Scriptures say in John 3:16? *"For God so loved the world that He gave His only begotten Son."* Think of the agony Christ had to experience, with overwhelming sadness and anguish in the garden of Gethsemane, knowing that [He] was going to be the sacrificial lamb for you and for me! **Where is your faith?** God shows us in the Gospels (according to Matthew, Mark, Luke, and John) the model for where our faith should be. He said to the *Father, "If it is possible, let this cup pass me by. Nevertheless, let it be as your will, not mine."* (Matthew 26:39)

This is our final point. **You got to work your faith!** James 2:14-26 gives you the full illustration of the text. In James 2 verse 21, we can see that Abraham, our father, was justified by his work (the act of doing something) when he offered his son Isaac on the altar. You got to see how Abraham's faith was working together with his work and by which his faith was made perfect.

God has allowed you to choose your mate and enter into the covenant with one another to fulfill the promises of being one. He will not force the two of you to walk in it and through it. Faith without works is dead. If you believe God has opened the door, and He does, the next step is up to the two of you!

The two of you need to go for it. Work out your faith and trust God! He is there for the two of you! Your marriage can be a true example of Christ and His love for the church. Trust that believing in Him, following His direction for your marriage, and placing Him at the head of your marriage will bring you a fulfilling covenant ordained by God.

We **TRUST** you to make the right decision to fight for your marriage!

iLOVE

"For God so loved the world that He gave His only begotten Son, that whosoever believeth in Him shall not perish but have everlasting life."
(John 3:16 NKJV)

Contributions by: Majid and Alesha Salahuddin

OUR LOVE STORY

The year was 1988, and we still remember it like it was yesterday. We met in high school and had been assigned to the same math class. The typical "boy meets girl" situation—a guy born and raised in Washington, D.C., meets the quiet, shy girl from the South. One was accustomed to girls that were somewhat *"fast"* and desired attention from the boys; the other one didn't have many friends. He says she caught his attention because she was so different from all the other girls.

Popular in high school and normally the center of attention (*star quarterback, student government president, a favorite amongst his teachers*), Majid could date anyone he chose. However, on the first day of class, he noticed this girl was different as she quietly sat in class, attentive to the teacher, ignoring the laughing and distractions from the other students. He wondered who she was and, why *she wasn't impressed with his jokes and overall class clowning like the other girls in class?* Majid's curiosity overwhelmed him to the point where he decided to make a move and engage her in conversation. He immediately fell in love with her *cute-shyness* and focused way of thinking. In addition, he loved the fact that she was not (at all) impressed with his status or position in high school. He decided to end the exchange by giving her his phone number to call him later on.

A couple of days later, Majid was on the balcony of a friend's house (which happened to face the terrace door of Alesha's house) when he saw her sister heading toward the door. He yelled down to her, ***"Hey, go get your sister for me!"*** so that's exactly what she did. In the next few moments, Alesha came out of the house and looked up at the balcony toward Majid, who proceeded to yell, ***"Why haven't you called me?"*** Alesha still remembers the mixed feelings she had at the time to this bold and assertive question, coming from a guy she barely knew!— feelings of anger (*because he was yelling so loud*), embarrassment (*I felt like everyone was looking out their windows because they could hear him yelling*), and laughter (*because he really didn't have a clue how to approach me!*) I decided to reply back with a flirty but curt, ***"Why didn't you call me—.you have my number as well?"*** The reply completely threw him off guard at this point, and Majid became obsessed with getting to know more about Alesha.

This was the same day Majid found out that Alesha was a teenage mom with a son who was barely three months old. Alesha remembered the other feelings of anxiousness and worry from this "surprise" visit from Majid because she knew he did not know she had a child. After her initial response to him on the balcony, she turned around and walked back into the house, causing him to rush down from his friend's house and knock on the door. After nervously answering the door, she knew there was no turning back and Majid would have to be told about her son. *"I was afraid of his response,"* she says. But after sharing her story, she became shocked at his response as he took her son in his arms and began bonding with him on the floor of her living room.

It was love at first sight! Majid felt like this was the day he knew Alesha was going to be his wife. So, after dating through high school, they were married in 1991, both at the tender age of eighteen years old. Majid joined the military, and the couple moved to North Carolina with their three young children. It was the first time both of us had been on our own, being so far away from our immediate family. Times were tough, living off a private's salary, caring for a severely disabled child and two other small children. We lived in a trailer home that was in less-than-ideal conditions. Struggling to pay bills was our way of life, and many times, something did not get paid. There was one time we couldn't afford to buy propane for the tank that supplied the trailer home with heat. We ended up sleeping with our coats on, bundling up in one bed to stay warm. Alesha remembers the day Majid became so frustrated with his inability to pay bills and take care of our growing family that he tried to send her back home to her mother's house. In no uncertain terms, she boldly told him "**NO!**" Through it all, we were determined to be together as husband and wife, even when we had every excuse to quit.

Now, we have been defined as a couple for over thirty years. God placed us together. He is the One who ordained our union as husband and wife—two heartbeats that became one; he is her heartbeat, and she is his.

LEARNING HOW TO LOVE

We can honestly say that we initially entered into our marriage committed to a deep desire to place each other's needs above our own. In the beginning, the intention was to make each other happy. However, we were very young, and some of our needs were not always met. We had not learned how to love the way God intended. Becoming husband and wife at the age of eighteen was extremely difficult. We weren't prepared for the responsibility that came with marriage. We were new to the role of having to love someone other than ourselves. Because of our immaturity, we made many mistakes in how we communicated daily with one another and how we interacted with each other during disagreements. We placed extreme demands on each other during the early days of our marriage.

At times, it was difficult for us as two teenagers to navigate the complex course of marriage. Our communication with each other wasn't always the best. Essentially, this caused many issues in our young marriage. Finances were another challenge that caused a different level of stress. Even intimacy, at times, was strained. We had not yet learned both the physical and emotional needs of a spouse. All of these issues impacted how we interacted with and communicated to one another.

However, it was our connection with our local church's marriage ministry that helped us truly understand covenant relationships. Once we joined the church, as a family, we gained a clear understanding of how marriage is indeed a ministry. What we were taught helped us define what it meant to be a husband and wife. The revelation of covenant relationships reinforced the positive in our marriage. We believe that the divine connection with our local church and the intentional effort to participate in marriage ministry were instrumental in our understanding of God's purpose and plan for our marriage and our lives.

Marriage is one of those things in which you should concentrate on being a better you. Many people spend their time in marriage pointing out their spouse's flaws. We learned that great marriages are those in which each person strives to be a better individual to perfect their union. We have replaced our personal agendas with one singular focus for our marriage. We aligned our individual goals to undergird the purpose and plan God has for us as one. Our marriage has a corporate vision for our house and our family. We continuously strive to see this vision come to pass on a daily basis.

As a military family, having a vision such as this was especially important. Frequent moves, long periods of separation, and the constant fear of deployments were a way of life. Many military marriages succumb to these challenges for one reason or another. However, we learned to love each other through it all. Again, we cite our connection with our local church as well as our personal relationships with God as a source of our fulfillment. Just as Jesus meets us right where we are in life, as husband and wife, we loved each other where *we* were in our marriage. Even though we both made mistakes, we learned to love each other through those mistakes.

This can be very difficult for some couples to do if both people in the marriage have not submitted to God's plan for their union. Learning to admit when we're wrong and apologize (*even when we do not feel like it*) have been keys to sustaining our love for over thirty years. We learned how to treat each other during both the good and bad times. Setting boundaries during arguments allows us to have *healthy* disagreements. Couples need to realize if you have offended your spouse or crossed the line in your communications, it is important to apologize. Humbling yourself and saying, "*I'm sorry,*" is one of the most helpful actions in a marriage. It shows a sign of strength, not weakness.

In addition to the act of apologizing, we have learned to exercise forgiveness. We have to forgive our spouse and leave the wrongdoing in the past where it belongs. Remember, communication is key. If you are someone who is having trouble doing this, ask God for His help and keep trying. You would want your spouse to do the same for you!

GOD'S COVENANT OF LOVE

In the book of John 3:16, we read of God's everlasting life covenant to us: *"For God so loved the world, that He gave His only begotten Son, that whosoever believeth in him should not perish, but have everlasting life."* God's covenant relationship with humanity shows us how He loved us so much that He sacrificed His only begotten Son! This covenant relationship reminds us of our marriage covenant, our vows we made to one another on our wedding day. What is a vow? It is defined as a solemn promise (an oath, a pledge, a bond, _covenant_, and commitment).

Marriage vows are the ultimate commitment by which husbands and wives pledge to one another all aspects of their lives—*"for better, for worse, for richer, for poorer, in sickness and in health, to love and to cherish, till death do us part."* This set of promises (covenant) is supposed to help set the tone and standard for how a marriage will flow—two people standing before God, vowing to love one another, be kind to one another, respect one another, be patient with one another, and value one another.

In today's society, there is no shortage of the world's version of what love should or shouldn't be. However, John 3:16 remains the single source and foundation for which our twenty-eight-year marriage has been built on. In Jesus's life, death, and resurrection, God revealed His desire to have a loving, covenant relationship with Him (and with one another). God initiated a covenant of love with us; it is our responsibility to fulfill that covenant by honoring each other in our marriage. Through our covenant in marriage, we were also offered the gift of identity. When we became husband and wife, this new identity became part of who we are and how we are known to others.

Imperfect as we are, each day we strive to emulate the unconditional love of Christ with acts of kindness, patience, forgiveness, selfless service to one another, and mutual love. Our marriage has required sacrifice. Those sacrifices have only magnified our love for one another over the years. Each day wasn't always enjoyable. In fact, some days we simply got on each other's nerves. But it is during those times where love is tested the most. The commitment to our covenant never waivers, and our love for one another grows and strengthens after each trial and test.

We are now able to tell young couples that our beautiful, love story is a byproduct of sacrifice and commitment. It seems that in this "microwave age," people want what they see in our marriage, but they don't want to go through the tests and trials or even sacrifice. It is the blessing of covenant that allows us to experience agape love—the type of love that Jesus Christ has for His people. Agape love is not swayed by feelings or emotions but the type of love that transcends all. A covenant marriage ties husband and wife together in a way that pledges mutual support, *the hope that the relationship will bring blessings as the couple continues on their life journey.*

OUR BLESSED FAMILY

Lastly, we understand that other than God, our family is the most important thing in our lives— being there for one another during good and bad times, encouraging one another, and unconditionally loving each other despite our faults. We know that our marriage serves as a great example for our children, their marriages, and the generations to come. Even when the demands of everyday life become great, we must never forget that we have been blessed with a wonderful family unit, and we share the responsibility of contributing to our family's emotional and spiritual well-being. We love each other hard and place God squarely in the center of our family life. Fellowship with one another is hugely important for our family. We love spending time with each other and sharing life's most precious moments. We thank God each day for blessing our marriage as well as our family. We believe it is His way of honoring the covenant we have with Him. Our love for each other is only surpassed by our love for God.

CONCLUSION

This book is a compilation of stories and testimonies from married couples, their journey together and how they have applied each of the *Recipe for Life* ingredients. We pray that this book blesses you and your marriage richly. This book is not designed to be a cure-all for everything that marriages may face but a tool, a resource, that can be drawn upon from real-life experience. Ask yourself, have you surrendered your will, have you trusted God, have you believed that God can do anything, have you loved like Christ, and do you still have hope in God and in your marriage?

> *Couples who mirror God's image experience oneness in their marriage (FamilyLife Weekend to Remember, 2020)*

If do not have a personal relationship with the Lord Jesus Christ, whether you are married, single, young, or old or you have turned your heart away from God and you are not a member of a church, then pray this prayer with us today:

> Dear Heavenly Father, I have lived my life without seeking You first. I have relied on my understanding, and I am wholeheartedly sorry. I admit that I am a sinner, and I surrender my life completely to You. I believe in my heart that You loved me enough to die for my sins, and now I forever put my trust and hope in You. In Jesus's name, Amen.

If you prayed this prayer and do not have a church home, we recommend that you find a church where they are preaching and teaching the gospel of Jesus Christ through the Holy Bible, where you can continue to grow in your personal relationship with Jesus Christ. What better day to start this journey than today.

CPSIA information can be obtained
at www.ICGtesting.com
Printed in the USA
LVHW081110130420
653235LV00016B/1296